SAINT AGNOSTICA

Winner of the L. E. Phillabaum Poetry Award for 2021

SAINT AGNOSTICA

ANYA KRUGOVOY SILVER

POEMS

LOUISIANA STATE UNIVERSITY PRESS
BATON ROUGE

Published by Louisiana State University Press
lsupress.org

Copyright © 2021 by Anya Krugovoy Silver
All rights reserved. Except in the case of brief quotations used in articles or reviews, no part of this publication may be reproduced or transmitted in any format or by any means without written permission of Louisiana State University Press.

LSU Press Paperback Original

DESIGNER: Michelle A. Neustrom
TYPEFACE: Calluna

COVER IMAGE: *From Nothing*, 2016, by Jeanie Tomanek

Thanks to the following journals where these poems were previously published: *32 Poems:* "The Dress Lamp Tree"; *About Place Journal:* "Nocturne with Spirits"; *Antioch Review:* "After a Nap"; *Chaleur Magazine:* "Born Melancholy" and "My Mother Buys Me Sea Salt"; *Christianity and Literature:* "Saint Peregrine" and "When"; *Crab Orchard Review:* "Eating Watermelon" and "Kindness"; *Five Points:* "All Souls Day," "Going," "In the College Woods," "Plunkett Pool," and "Reading Poetry in Illness"; *Georgia Review:* "Among the Losses" and "Poetry Class, Ash Wednesday"; *Green Mountains Review:* "You and I Are Earth"; *Hudson Review:* "'Knowing What You Know Now, Would You Choose to Be Born?'" and "Sacred Moments"; *Hypertext Magazine:* "Amazement," "Meditation on a Thirteenth Century Icon," and "September"; *Immanence Journal:* "The Work"; *Missouri Review:* "At the Peak," "Crow's Funeral," "Hunted," "My Son's Abs," "Panic Attack," and "Red Tulips in Red Jug, Haarlem"; *Ploughshares:* "Being Ill"; *Quiet* Storm: "Brain Scan on Yom Kippur"; *Southern Review:* "Disappearances," "How to Tie a Chemo Scarf," and "National Radio Quiet Zone." "Kindness" also appeared in *Healing the Divide: Poems of Kindness and Connection*, ed. James Crews.

LIBRARY OF CONGRESS CATALOGING-IN-PUBLICATION DATA

Names: Silver, Anya Krugovoy, 1968–2018, author.
Title: Saint Agnostica : poems / Anya Krugovoy Silver.
Description: Baton Rouge : Louisiana State University Press, [2021] | "LSU Press paperback original"—Title page verso.
Identifiers: LCCN 2021001333 (print) | LCCN 2021001334 (ebook) | ISBN 978-0-8071-7565-1 (paperback) | ISBN 978-0-8071-7637-5 (pdf) | ISBN 978-0-8071-7638-2 (epub)
Subjects: LCGFT: Poetry.
Classification: LCC PS3619.I5465 S25 2021 (print) | LCC PS3619.I5465 (ebook) | DDC 811/.6—dc23
LC record available at https://lccn.loc.gov/2021001333
LC ebook record available at https://lccn.loc.gov/202100133

You will hear thunder and remember me and think—she wanted storms.

—ANNA AKHMATOVA

CONTENTS

Elegy *1*

I

Hunted *5*
Brain Scan on Yom Kippur *6*
September *7*
Stray Elk in Église Saint-Eustache *8*
"So Look, So See!" *9*
All Souls Day *10*
Lessons and Carols, Advent *11*
You and I are Earth *12*
Born Melancholy *13*
In the College Woods *15*
Meditation on a Thirteenth-Century Icon *16*
Among the Losses *17*
At the Peak *18*

II

How to Tie a Chemo Scarf *21*
Red Tulips in Red Jug, Haarlem *23*
Saint Peregrine *24*
Saint Agnostica *25*
Three Songs for Doubt *26*
On the Existence of Evil *27*
When *28*
Poetry Class, Ash Wednesday *29*
Being Ill *30*
Hating the Healthy Poets *31*
Poem for Dr. ——— *32*
Lana Del Rey's Scream *33*
Turban *34*

III

Costly Love 37
Sacred Moments 38
Open 39
Plunkett Pool 40
After Swimming 41
My Son's Abs 42
An Outline (Possible) 43
My Mother Buys Me Sea Salt 44
Kindness 45
Amazement 46
The Dress Lamp Tree 47
Eating Watermelon 48
Home Repairs 49
Going 50

IV

"Knowing What You Know Now, Would You Choose to be Born?" 53
After a Nap 54
Nocturne with Spirits 55
Disappearances 56
National Radio Quiet Zone 57
Reading Poetry in Illness 58
The Work 59
The Last Happy Day 60
Chimney Swifts 62
Panic Attack 63
Klonopine 65
Unfinished 66
Metastatic 67
Crow's Funeral 68

ACKNOWLEDGMENTS 71

SAINT AGNOSTICA

ELEGY

Not for me, but for all the others, the *intolerably
nameless names,* the conscription into disease
and death, the further obscenity of forgetfulness.
The terrible slowness or appalling swiftness,
neither easier than the other, just different tortures.
To eulogize them all, an impossible task.
Memory refuses. Self-preservation balks.
The knowledge, not to be denied, that I too
will be the one about whom the living speak someday.
Better beat a drum or swell the strings
with a Beethoven sonata. Any adagio, minor key.
Or drape myself with scarves and dance barefoot,
arms outstretched, head fallen backwards, taut throat.
Better just be silent. What I could write, I wrote.

1

HUNTED

Imagine being hunted—poached, illegally,
knowing how much someone desires you,
wants your body, will never stop stalking you
with whatever weapons he devises.
Camouflaged, utterly silent, relentless,
a hunter who would burn the very tusks he seeks,
would flay the hide that makes the quarry valuable.
And you know you're being hunted—
every week, you come upon new corpses,
not only the weak and old among you,
but also the most determined, the fiercest
of your kind, caught up in a net they'd never seen.
Eventually, you will leave the tribe,
decimated as it is, always mourning and fearful.
You will walk to a lake, or a field,
someplace you find peaceful and beautiful,
and simply lie down there,
putting aside any of your last defenses.
You'll wait for him to find you,
knowing there is no escape anyway,
hoping to get a bullet to the head
before he removes the knives from his sack,
with which he will extract the organs
from your body, one by one.

BRAIN SCAN ON YOM KIPPUR

Lying masked in the tube,
I close my eyes and let the buzz
tune my mind to half-trance, half-sleep.
In the synagogue, the congregation prays
in Hebrew, a language I don't speak.
In the MRI, the banging, pinging coils
chant their own tongue of film and slice.
I'm not fasting. The IV feeds dye
into my vein, which sends it to cranial folds.
As the lens searches my brain for tumors,
I imagine God's eye scanning my soul.
Don't move. Lie perfectly still, the tech says.
And so I wait, shrouded in the tunnel,
as ink dries on the divine scroll,
and the Gates begin to close.

SEPTEMBER

What's this hair drifting from my scalp?
Why do my fingers pass over my nape
and pull away a fist of strands?
Why is my head mimicking autumn
by shedding itself all over the rugs,
my sweaters, the book in my lap?
What is this doughy face in the mirror,
a bald spot erasing my once slender part?
And what's to be done with all this hair
floating into my son's food, settling on armchairs?
And why is it wet, sometimes? Tell me.

STRAY ELK IN ÉGLISE SAINT-EUSTACHE

The elk strolls through the church,
his antlers enormous, inverted chandeliers.
He steps up, then down, from the altar.
Against his soft brown, the grey marble's
glow seems less earthly. His hooves ring.
He moves his head slowly back and forth,
as though looking for something he needs
He sniffs the font, but does not drink.
Like a prince enchanted in an old tale,
the elk stands completely himself in a place
where he does not belong.
No wonder so many poets have seen the face
of an animal and thought of Jesus. How easy
to pray to something strange, ineffable,
something that pays you no attention.

"SO LOOK, SO SEE!"

line from a poem by Joachim Ringelnatz

How little looking I do—
this early autumn could skitter by
with scant notice. But my pen
grounds me like a plum line.

I'm lucky to hold it,
to sit with a pad of lined paper.
Otherwise, I wouldn't note the grackles
in the neighbor's water oaks,
camouflaged in leaves still thick and green.
I might not have squeezed the black mulch
in the trunk of the fallen tree, dark and moist
as chocolate cake.

Today, the sunbeam on the folded rug
relaxes its spine into faded wool.
My dog lies, in total trust, on her back.

I don't know what bliss is,
but it could be as simple as late
September, this chewed-up armchair,
memory of summer, and my pen and paper—
an inexpressible fortune.

ALL SOULS DAY

No ancient tricks have staved my illness off—
no hollow head placed grinning on the steps,
or amulet I've dipped in holy springs.

The earth's a scab of stubbled wheat and rye.
I take the month as my motif and lie
in bed this evening, weeping and alone.

And now I feel them come, these gathering souls.
They fill the twilit room like drifting seeds,
their pity, strained of human pity's gall.

I offer them my living warmth—my hands,
my face, my heart's release—and take from them
the grace they leave: this temporary peace.

LESSONS AND CAROLS, ADVENT

I'm told that light meets the darkness
and is not overcome. But I am overcome,
again and again, each day a stumble into grief.
I want to slap the maudlin out of myself.
Where has my fearlessness gone?
Where is the owl that once perched on my wrist?
My husband curls his arm round my waist.
Woe, world-sorrow. I long for so much.
Angels fly around the church dome
as if this world didn't belong to sparrows.

YOU AND I ARE EARTH

inscription on an English plate, 1661

You and I are earth.
Maybe that's why I crave mountains
as though they were holy places,
my mind a meadow worshipping in asters.

I crave mountains with the old hope
that their heights could save me,
my mind a meadow worshipping in asters,
pulling through meager roots my resurrection.

If those heights could save me,
could lend me their slow, fissured years,
I would delay disease, delay my death,
draw changelessness from granite.

If mountains could lend me their slow years,
their icy peaks and withholding pastures,
I could live changeless as the granite
and not, like you and I, as earth.

BORN MELANCHOLY

after Mary Szybist

Having been born melancholy, I love the hyacinth
scent of its dusty, gold-stamped spine.

My father's repeated stories, the *Bozhe Moy*
shaking of his head at the supper table,
his bent back seen from outside the house
when he sat on the couch, always waiting,
or remembering, or worrying about something he'd lost.

Being born melancholy, I accepted as normal
my grandmother's self-imposed exile and martyrdom
in the corner bedroom, where she stored her toaster
oven, icons, and anatomy books.

The Slavic chanting in church both bored and tired,
but, unlike American hymns, did not annoy me.

Early on, I gravitated to boy singers who smudged their eyes
and posed on bluffs like Heathcliffs in pluming sleeves.

I like the denseness and thickness of melancholy,
its mossy thickets.

When I married my husband, we joined our melancholies
together, and for that reason, understand each other always.

The bow of forehead to floor, the communion wine
bursting Joy's grape against my palate—
I could sleep in melancholy's deepest blue for days.

Sometimes, melancholy and happiness twin through my body,
a twining moon flower, double locket with an opal frame.

My mouth tastes of thistle and cloves, or the coffee rinds left in the bottom of a cup of Turkish coffee.

Winter evenings, I'm glad to ease my mind from the sun.

IN THE COLLEGE WOODS

for Andy

Christmas evening, as we walked the woods,
two deer, a doe and stag, suddenly zig-
zagged in front of my husband and me,
vanishing in a swag of white and tan.
We hadn't heard them, hadn't seen them
in the spruce along the darkening path.
Yet, there they were—miracles of quiet
and quickness, of coupled wildness.
It was twilight already, the rooms lit
in the one house at the path's end.

MEDITATION ON A THIRTEENTH-CENTURY ICON

Oil and flame have darkened the faces
of the saints, their bodies dimmed
till all that's left are sweeping
robes, naked feet, and haloed heads.
Compline chants and flickers.
Staring at these nameless women,
the hush between us thickens.
Mere soot against gilded wood,
they offer no tokens, no signs.
Nothing frightens them,
neither time nor decay.
I wither, like a blue gentian
ashed to black, and pray.

AMONG THE LOSSES

My lamentations have shaken loose locusts.
They whir in the burned-out nave of my body.

In the shower, whole decades wash from my body.
A girl's hairless limbs emerge naked from the spray.

Among the losses: tube tops, demicups, skin-kissing
chocolate lace. Dreamy clutter of the desired body.

Obsessively, I imagine Christmas photographs without me.
Gold and crimson. My son. Another woman's body.

Among the losses: death as metaphor, as my body
floating in salt waves, carried back to the waters.

Many days, I want to throw my fists against God's body.
But nothing, nothing.

Hold me, all you saints and angels. Don't let life,
like a child struggling in my arms, climb out of my body.

AT THE PEAK

In Brienz, I took a steam engine
so far up a mountain I passed clouds
and the shy goats that live too far
up the gouged granite to tame.
Once out of the train, the thin air
kept my lungs from climbing higher.
Alpine ranges hammocked me
like folds of silk on a saint's lap.
The mountains shrank me to rock jasmine,
lavender petals creeping in the cliffs.
A friend once told me, "Women are stronger
than a firing squad." I stood by the rail
knowing the bullets have left the chambers.

II

HOW TO TIE A CHEMO SCARF

Close the door and stand before a mirror.
Cup your face in your hands,
nesting your cheeks in your palms.
Admire the shape of your skull.
It vessels whatever you are.

Somewhere in your brain, memories
stir, flowing to the foreground.
All your humours are cranial.

Your hair rarely looked the way you liked it,
but remember its best days:
when a stylist sprayed the long strands
around soda can-sized rollers,
then backcombed a bouffant.
Feel your curls soften and glide,
dark shine between oiled fingers.

Realize that, as an object of desire,
you will walk invisibly mile after mile.
Yet, wherever you go, people will gawk
at you without pity, just curiosity.

Or worse, with pity.

When you feel alone, line your lips bloody.
Clip the chunkiest hoops to your lobes.

Death, what of it? It was always there.
Your gaze is just sharper now.
If you want to curse, curse.

Then picture a split-open geode,
its quartz exposed and radiant.

Now, pick up your scarf.

RED TULIPS IN RED JUG, HAARLEM

painting by Winifred Nicholson

One day, red wracked me,
ripped me open seam to seam,
and overcame me, said:
Girl—crash, knock over, spill.
Give name to. Be merciless.
At first, I held out against it,
wanting only the calm sky,
immersion, Vermeer's robe.
But red thrust its iron brush
in my hand so my words
would rush, reveal, heal,
the way a blood transfusion
once made me feel winged
and hot, holding out for glory
my wondrous wounds.

SAINT PEREGRINE

Cleaning and sorting her mother's boxes,
my friend found a medal of Saint Peregrine,
patron saint of those with AIDS and cancer.
She was embarrassed to offer it to me,
dusty bit of folk belief and superstition.
But of course I wanted it. Her mother,
I don't know how, pushing the pendant
forward for her daughter to notice
among cocktail rings and brooches.
The medal, wanting to be touched,
for the oil of fingers to rub back its shine.
Clutter of wishes—angel pins, saints' cards,
bags of prayer shawls—haven't saved me.
But I'd like a saint of my own,
with a name as strange as the names of medications.
I slip the medallion in the pocket of my jeans,
a coin to use for the crossing.

SAINT AGNOSTICA

Where's the saint of doubt I need?
Does she exist, Saint Agnostica,
with an annotated Bible and eye
for dogmatic nonsense?
I imagine that she wears denim,
toys with mysticism, is drawn to Camus.
She formulates proofs for God
in a notebook, alongside shopping lists.
Saint Agnostica might explain to me
why worship no longer bends my knees.
She would understand my love of incense
and the Eucharist, and my lack of concern
for the Creed, which I mutter through
with folded hands while gazing at a corner.
She might make me feel less guilty
for packing my purse during post-
Communion prayers and thanks.
She would understand my desire to love God,
but shrug when I say I'm not sure I do.
She's a smart saint, canny but indecisive.
When she takes me for coffee,
she can't decide between black or cream.
She craves sugar, but drinks her brew bitter.

THREE SONGS FOR DOUBT

i.

No longer believing was easy as eating pudding.
All of a sudden, I was roused.
I no longer needed God to house my suffering.
Life became its own meaning.
I ebbed into unbelief so easily,
letting thought ease my fall.
It was a relief, setting faith free.

ii.

The day I starting doubting,
a priest thanked God he wasn't poor.
He praised the Lord who raised up America.
Peru, he said, lacked civilization.
The faithful kneeled around me
to accept the beaten body of Christ.
For the first time, I didn't kneel.
Unbelief came upon me like a wind
and held me like I'd always hoped that God would.

iii.

Take the world's beauty as given, not conclusion.
Now start withholding.
Deduct trafficked girls, missile strikes, ALS.
Write the evidence for God's presence on the board
as you once stood in front of the classroom,
trying to decode the geometric proof.
Not figuring it out doesn't mean you've failed.
Scratch out God. Now solve the problem.

ON THE EXISTENCE OF EVIL

Adam and Eve are my favorite
excuse for suffering. "They ate
the fruit of the tree and were expelled
from Paradise." Oh, luminous eyes!
Oh, blank spaces! Bless your
innocence. Your unbloodiedness.
The clean slicing open of sin
like a tinned ham. The Second Coming.
If the world is falling by our own doing,
do not worry. Humans, take your dioxins,
the lead in the soil. Hew to God's plan.
Praise the gather and the wither.

WHEN

When everything happens for a reason,
I'll unpeel the seed pods in my throat.
Relieved, I'll thread a pair of scissors
into my lungs and snip open the egg sacs
that have nestled in the pleural lining.
I'll believe all the bruises.
I'll untwist bottles of anger capsules
so the tiny pink balls inside can roll away.
The clip-on bangs will scuttle under the bed.
When everything happens for a reason,
I'll reach my fists into the valleys
and stretch them like taffy into peaks.
Each one will be named for a woman.
Glamour. Dickinson. Hallucination. Root.

POETRY CLASS, ASH WEDNESDAY

> Your death questions my life.
> —JOHANNES BOBROWSKI

I store the empty bottle of maple syrup
Kristin tapped in '12 (her last) in the fridge door.
Sweet William Amber, she'd written on the label.
She loved Emily Dickinson, England, and bonfires.
Death was a cold broth. Sickness spread
through her bones like burrs on socks.
No peace, no atonement, no relief.
I want everyone to understand the grief.
There is no happy turn, no radiant *volta*.
I won't offer a lit lantern or fist of violets.
One of my students stays after class.
What do you mean by dust to dust?
she asks me—curious rabbit, owlet.
My smile's vulpine. *I mean you, girl. Us.*

BEING ILL

There's no heroism to it.
Like getting dressed in the morning,
it's just practice: force my head past the collar,
squiggle to pull up the zipper
behind my back, slither into tights
and distinguish blue pumps from black.
I pour the cereal in my bowl the same way
each morning because that's how it's done—
life, the whole scribbled mess of it.
There's no bravery in habit.
Even waiting for the doctor to arrive,
knowing she's holding scan results,
requires no striving, no grand strength.
I'm just a limp sock in a dog's mouth.
Fate drops me in my life and I land.
It's the only way I know to survive.

HATING THE HEALTHY POETS

God, give me patience with these healthy poets.
They write of illness like priests explaining the Trinity,
or children mispronouncing letters—*my bwotha
wath thick today*—not knowing how to curl their tongues.
Lord, shut up these poets. Stop their pens.
Let there be exceptions only for those who humble themselves
before the mystery, who crawl like communicants
across a terrain they do not understand, who willingly dig
beneath the peat to find the end of the fern's long foot,
who will rock on their feet, pulling and pulling,
straining their thighs until they fall back, sweating,
the plant in their laps. Then, and only then,
should they write down the first word. Only one.
They must repeat the process till the entire poem is done.

POEM FOR DR. ——

> Smear me / with black rage / from head to toe.
> —MIKLÓS RADNÓTI

Tear up the sad page. Rip its stitching
from my book. Ink over its watery lines.
Untwist the lids from my tubes of blood
and pour them down the front of my gown.
Mark me gruesome. Now bring in the doctor.
Let her tell me again that my treatment
is a *crapshoot.* Let me hear her say
Six months is better than nothing, then shrug.
This time I will not reach for the tissues
she carelessly flicks toward me.
Rather, I'll lean toward her face and scream.
One long, Munch-like howl.
I want to watch her face turn human.
Let her smell the meat of me, the wick.

LANA DEL REY'S SCREAM

Lana Del Rey crawls through the desert.
Lana Del Rey's white t-shirt dips off her shoulder.
Lana Del Rey screams as loudly as she can into the face of a biker.
Into the sky. Against the fire. At the *broken stars*.
Her scream hurtles into the abyss and is digitized as a song.
Soon, Lana is wearing blue and white roses in her hair,
a diamond tooth cap, and a ring that reads "Bad."
Lana winks like a pinup in front of the American flag.
Lana croons about furs and guns, briefly goes bouffant.
Eventually, the scream is labeled "iconic," disappears
into Instagram, gains Grammy nominations, goes cosmic.
Lana Del Rey poses as Mary with a pierced heart
(Gucci Haute Couture). Critics can be so mean sometimes.
On stage, Lana smiles and drops to a squat like a glacier.
She sings the word *bitch* in the pitch of a lullaby.
It's midnight. The desert is still the desert.
Truckers drive through the quiet. Lana screams.
She's still there, on her knees.
I have climbed through the scream, a torn-open screen.
It's not real, but it's true.

TURBAN

Step away from the door.
I am a battering ram. I go where I want.
My birch legs leap between now and now,
each moment seven days of creation.
I ride my stone bowl through the night.
The holes in my bones are studded with rubies.
I live both blue and red.
Both dead and true. Always raging,
always riding winter's breath.
I despise health and all that is easy.
Watch me at the mirror wrapping my skull
in satin, winding it closely around a pillow
that rises from my head like a pillar.
I wrap it till I'm a foot taller,
antlered, cantilevered.
I walk through my fear like a robed
priest through incense: whatever is offered
to God is holy. I am that offering.

III

COSTLY LOVE

It's costly, the love I bear my son.
Without it, I could easily finger
each hydrocodone from its bottle,
count them like rosary beads
while swallowing them down,
a body consuming its prayer.

And my love for my husband,
that too is costly—
it prevents a quick jump
from the bridge (I've picked
the place) above the railroad tracks,
where I could watch oncoming lights
with plenty of chances a day.

Love is not free or unbounded
from demands I'd rather not meet:

the deep, daily exhaustion, hours of naps,
pain that laps at each passage of the body
and fills it with cramping smoke.

Hours spent each week in a recliner,
accepting poisons that slowly destroy me.

Each day, I flip a new coin
into love's bag.

I continue to pay the cost:
a sag in my spine, the long wait until bedtime.

SACRED MOMENTS

One evening, I lay on my stomach, weeping,
wondering at what moment death would come.
My brain heated like broth, shaking the lid of the pot.
The only thing that calmed me down was my son's voice,
narrating a Lego battle in his bedroom.
It was a day of doom, with many casualties.
I lay still and thought, *I have you, you, you,*
though my son wasn't even aware that I listened,
or that I had lost control of the motions of my face.
Somehow, I summoned the spirits of my sisters,
who sat in the bed with me and waited, silent webs,
till I was calm enough to get up and leave the room.

OPEN

> Our heart is wide open to you. There is no restriction in our affections, but only in yours. In return—I speak as to children—open wide your heart also.
>
> —2 CORINTHIANS 6: 11–13

My heart narrows and narrows,
like the Rio Grande pinched between cliffs,
like any wide path suddenly ruined in rubble.
I shouldn't be able to count the people
whom I love on my fingers.
In a photograph, a child stands and wails
for his mother, rejecting the stiff, strange
sleeves that reach for him.
Love gashes the scarred heart,
takes on the patterns of pain
and hopelessness, the helplessness I felt
carrying my infant son for hours
as he wailed and I couldn't comfort him,
wanting nothing more myself than sleep.
Yet, when I tired and put him down,
he held his arms out for what comfort
I could offer. Whoever thinks of love
as happiness hasn't really felt it.

PLUNKETT POOL

My son wants me to watch his underwater flips.
After he vaults off the diving board,
he looks over to make sure I've seen.
My attention won't matter much longer.
He's already asked me not to meet him after school,
makes a rule of walking in front of me
(the ruse of all fourteen year olds).
But this June, he still squints at me
when his face breaks through the water.
He smiles at my thumbs-ups, then plunges
again beneath the pool's blue surface,
that looks so clear and familiar
but is, I know, an element
that I will never comprehend.

AFTER SWIMMING

My niece's pony tail's a skinny lanyard
as she climbs from the pool—
soaked hair, false blue water,
the way blonde threads will darken
when drenched, and lose their fullness.
All the silly dances in the living room—
her arms whirling like eggbeaters,
hips whipping left to right,
slick summer light off her cheek—
I'm watching my past dancing,
little slip of childhood, like bit of shine.
And when adolescence closes over her head,
will the thread of her voice be broken?
Will her sentences float up at the end
like mine did, phrased as blameless questions?
Will she waste hours yielding herself
to the glossy lip and tape measure?
(As I did, and my friend, and my friend before her.)
Or will she break the surface streaming, prismatic,
humming, her own voice gathered, gem-
like, statement and reply?

MY SON'S ABS

At fourteen, his voice and waistband drop.
He's stopped smiling for photos,
and I'm no longer welcome to rifle his hair.
Tonight, he asks me to punch his abs.
The boy still calls me *mama* when he's sad,
but he's crunching his core.
Because I won't hit him, even in sport,
he balls up my fist in his,
and twists my arm towards him.
His muscles are new, unfamiliar
on the child who so recently climbed
into bed with me after a nightmare.
Now I've changed his curtains
from dayglow yellow to solid blue.
I don't have the common sense to let him grow.
And after the abs, what comes next?
A razor, license, sorrows he won't share?
I ask him where he's going. He shrugs
and wrings the boyhood from his skin.

AN OUTLINE (POSSIBLE)

I draw an outline for my life.
Of course, these are only estimates.

3–6 months on X—
by then it will be August.

I will watch my son turn fourteen.
This year, I'll bake the cake myself.

3 months on Y *if* I can get it.
(No guarantee that I can get it.)

If I do, I'll celebrate my fiftieth
and one last fir in the foyer.

After that, there's probably Z.
Give or take three months.

Then it'll really be shit.
Exhausted, with nothing left to try.

Still, maybe I'll stretch my life
a couple of months longer

so I'm alive when my son turns fifteen.
Of course, these are only estimates.

MY MOTHER BUYS ME SEA SALT

in bottles and plastic bags,
crystals grey, pink, and red,
in addition to the common white.
I have grown doe-ish, pinch it
from the jar, lick it from my fingers,
sow it over everything I eat.
I think of amniotic fluid in which
I was immersed for nine months.
I remember my grandmother throwing salt
over her shoulder against the evil eye.
Lot's wife, a pillar pelted with wind
until she wore down to a pitted mound.
I think of ruin. I think, encrustation.
The rut of tears down my cheeks.
I brush my legs with salt to uncover luster.
I store it in its own wooden ark.
My mother's salt savors the food I eat.
It testifies to the holy of holies.

KINDNESS

Last week, a nurse pulled a warm blanket
from a magical cave of heated cotton
and lay it on my lap, even wrapping
my feet. She admired my red sandals.
Once, a friend brought me a chicken
she'd roasted and packed with whole lemons.
I ate it with my fingers while it was still warm.
Kindnesses appear, then disappear so quickly
that I forget their brief streaks: they vanish,
while cruelty pearls its durable shell.
Goodness streams like hot water through my hair
and down my skin, and I'm able to live
again with the ache. Love wakens the world.
Kindness is my mother, sending me a yellow dress in the mail
for no reason other than to watch me twirl.

EATING WATERMELON

Field of grounded green moons,
tethered to the earth with veined vines,
some of them waxing and waning,
some of them full Thunder moons,
their streaks stretch marks.
(*Did you swallow a watermelon seed?*
I once asked a pregnant woman.)
The watermelon is all head, all belly,
perfectly sealed against incursions.
It wants to be opened, my husband says.
So, with a huge knife, he halves it
till the two sides cleave, bloody starred
universes, staining white cotton shirts.
Easily sliced with dental floss,
it unfolds its wholeness into triangles.
We eat the entire melon in a day.
I cube it in a bowl, my husband gnaws
down to the rind, my son is lavishly
wasteful, then turns the shell into a mask
with which to chase the bored dog.
All that's left on the counter
are translucent scraps and corners.
My love and I scoop out the bits
with wet and sugary fingers.

AMAZEMENT

Marvelous that my mother found a batch
of seeds that her father, before he died
in '96, had carefully bound in paper.

My German grandfather, who tended
marigolds and roses, clipped hedgerows,
never liked to throw a useful thing away.

Amazing that, on being sown, the seeds
sprang into rangy orange cosmos, a sunset
hue not often seen in these wild blooms.

Now the German flowers blaze
on my mother's apartment balcony,
immigrants like she was fifty years ago.

Roughness has not destroyed them.
Beneath their tough shells, tendrils waited
for the urgent pull of sun on soil.

How long can tenderness survive a dark hull?
Touching the petals, a dullness lifts from my face.
I am still awake.

THE DRESS LAMP TREE

photograph by Tim Walker

On the tree hang twelve party dresses:
bell-skirted, ruffled, pouf-sleeved,
all lit from within by hidden bulbs
so their mint-green, turquoise, apricot
and yellow glow like underworld princesses,
or the spirits of long-shuttered ballrooms.
If I walked naked beneath the tree,
one of the gowns would drop on my bare skin,
lift me from the earth, the too solid earth,
and I'd become the cherry spirit of this July night.
Young again, hair tumbled past my shoulders,
my throat long and taut like a stem.
I'd whisper the ballads that I'm too old for,
Just put your sweet kiss, kiss on my lips now baby.

HOME REPAIRS

Our house is rotting around us.
The carpenter pokes his finger in the porch eaves
and a whole piece of fascia board swings
down like a disturbed bat.
He chuckles as he rambles around the house,
noting the broken window (into which a boy
crashed his tricycle a decade ago),
the clogged gutters in which a miniature pine
has rooted herself into rich brown mulch.
The pecan branches bend towards the roof,
a dancer who longs to collapse into his partner.
The bill comes to $8,000. The last of our small
inheritance scuttles through the porch fissures.
"You know, some neighbors would call the police
on a house like this," he adds.
But there's so much he hasn't calculated:
how vines growing over the side of the house
shadow the study so we can read in the morning,
how much I love the fat purple crepe myrtle
blossoms knocking against the bathroom window,
and the way one loose board rattles in wind
as though there were a mouse scratching at the sill
(and there have been mice, a family, in our sofa).
For over a hundred years, these rooms have held in,
kept out, muffled arguments, darkened for love making.
Our house is not an iced cake, but a cobbler, buckle,
crisp, dump cake, slump. A mess of peach slices,
strawberries, blueberries, however much brown sugar
and cinnamon are left in the cabinets, spoonfuls of butter.
"Never mind what it looks like," I might say,
handing a warn bowl to a guest. "But first,
let me put on a scoop of vanilla ice cream for flavor."

GOING

Before she left, she secured her boy in a boat
and chanted to him the ancient myths.
He slept, but she pressed her forehead
to his, so he would hear her words in dreams.
It grew darker; the fever had broken.
The house was hushed, it let her go.
The wind's damp lashes lifted her.
She rose, searching for a break in the sky.

IV

"KNOWING WHAT YOU KNOW NOW, WOULD YOU CHOOSE TO BE BORN?"

Don't say *no* out loud. Don't admit
that gold-sponged April isn't enough,
that the first milky sip of coffee or fuchsia
bougainvillea on a Greek patio don't provide
moments that make life worth its worry.

Such reflection belies the plaques in each
cheap beachside shop that remind us
to be merry, or what fun we should feel,
even about the small, sappy ways we go wrong.
The world demands our sloppy awe.

I've been struck down too many times.
Stuck, poisoned, drained, radiated fourteen years.
Truly, if not for love, I would choose oblivion.
Sweet love, a stone jammed in my jaw.

AFTER A NAP

When I woke up,
I was so far into dreaming
that I'd forgotten who I was.

So far into dreaming,
that I couldn't remember my name,
or whether or not I was single.

I couldn't remember my name,
so I concentrated on myself,
and finally returned to my mind:

I concentrated on myself, said aloud,
"You're Anya, you have cancer, you're married,"
and then all the beads fell back in place.

"You're Anya, you have cancer, you're married."
My name, my health, my love.
The knowledge I'll forget all this forever.

Soon, I'll forget all this forever,
going even more deeply into dreams:
where to, I can't say—but far, far.

NOCTURNE WITH SPIRITS

Thunder clouds blacken the blue sky.
The flower moon's dimmed.
Impossible not to sense ghosts in the trees.
The branches try to shake them off.
If I could only see what can't be seen.
The poor dimensions of my sight.
The defiant dead.
Night sky flushed and richly dark.
I'm not crazy—the wind's strange.
I wish I could illuminate time,
could pull down its edges.
All my dead sisters would return
and I would open my house to them.
I don't fear what once was good.

DISAPPEARANCES

When a voice stops talking, it simply stops.
Once the room was full, every chair occupied.
No matter how late I stayed up,
another woman somewhere was cleaning her kitchen.
Even when they disappeared one by one,
their last messages innocuous, unaware
that they were the last, I remained in the room.

I tried to seal it off, once,
like my husband tried to cap the chimney.
But the birds keep tumbling down the bricks.
The last one hadn't even grown feathers, still fetal.
Just so, I let one last woman in.
For a year, we talked to each other
and forgot the time, forgot its relentless leak.
One morning, I tried to write her, but she had suddenly died.

With every death, the room I sit in empties.
The curtains, the rug, the lamp, the loveseat.
Now it's just me in my favorite chair,
with no one to talk to. I wait
for the force that will pull me from the chair,
for the room's blankness to draw me under
—the way my son
observed when he was four, *human beings are balloons,*
no hands or legs, just big bellies,
with no control over where the wind pushes them.

NATIONAL RADIO QUIET ZONE

Green Bank, West Virginia

Here there are no *crystals, chimes,* or *twinkles.*
No *bamboo, chords, popcorn,* or *synth.*
No ringtones at all. No blinking apps.

Only landlines, with their quaint, curled cords,
interrupt the day's work and the evening's rap
of tableware, the glide of a finger along a page.

Imagine the muting of digital clamor—
hearing, instead, the cracks, barks, and snaps
of the half-hidden world, the movement of things.

To pay more attention to the clicking of water
in a shower, the swish of a brush through hair,
the velvet give of yogurt when stirred with a spoon.

Quiet draws me deeply—it's why
I go slack in a lake with my ears underwater,
or attend to the slow unwinding of cicada song.

I want silence to gather me into itself,
for stars and love to move in closer,
to unwrap my voice and hear it clearly, at last.

READING POETRY IN ILLNESS

Certain names are sacred to me.
I no longer waste time on books
that don't wrestle with angels,
leaving my fingers bruised
as I turn the pages of slim volumes.
The great ones—only regular humans,
with the same problems as thousands
before or since. But God took them
and held them before a dry wind,
and their helpless bodies swallowed
all the swirling sand, rocks, and blood,
and from this, poems forced their way.
I won't mention their names,
lest their spirits recoil at praise.
But the lashes on my skin that their words
have left—see how they flash golden,
like the spot where the enchanted bear's pelt
has been ripped away by a briar.

THE WORK

> It is not ours to finish the work but also not ours to abandon it.
> —RABBI TUPHON

Even if I live to be two hundred,
like some Biblical matriarch,
there would not be time to write
down everything I want to write down,
not time even to catalog the details
of a single room: in mine, I note
my great-aunt's ivory brooch, a burned-
out fir-scented votive, a pile of blankets
needing washing after my son's sickness,
and my son's knees, bent as he reads on the bed.
I could keep writing, on and on,
each moment its own universe to memorialize,
but since time is never enough (cracked tile,
bottle of blue nail polish, double-stacked books),
there's less sorrow in not having enough of it.
No completing the work, the poems,
those fur-faced bats that swoop and quiver.
But I can't stop—can't let future grief
still the pen, or let worry shackle
my wrist's quick stammer across the page.
God sees everything. Or God doesn't.
Who knows? I want to be like the icon
my father visited, the Mary who wept oil.
All the world's oil, someone must weep it.

THE LAST HAPPY DAY

when when when will it be   o world
I know it's coming, feel it,   autumn, winter,
maybe spring   after all, I can't be sure,
or even if it already was, not in morning but twilight,

1) blue blouse
2) flowers on table at all times
3) stack of favorite poetry
4) coffee in the freezer
5) music

also: quiet
also: paying attention

my doctor says   *you have a few options remaining::*

so in case I've had the last
I write down what I want to remember:

Tschüsseli, at the airport, blackberry tart with cream,
the granite peak's cocked hat, stacked patterns of firewood,
fuschia bottlebrushes growing alongside the river,
and my husband and me side by side in the attached twins,
looking up at the wooden ceiling listening to my breath,
feeling summer summer summer.

(*Tschüsseli,* I'd like to keep that.)

Just in case those were the last happiest days::

do you want me to tell you how many months?
Is that really a conversation you want to have right now?::

Play me adagios, whatever is retrievable

Before me, there's something:: behind me, everything

CHIMNEY SWIFTS

The swifts that nest in our chimney
protest, clamor, screech their needs.
They interrupt my morning coffee
with raucous bickering and bawling
in their crumbling tower of hunger,
doing the difficult work of climbing
and fledging in a constrained world.
At the same time, only in the narrow
flues can they develop, learn to sing.
When they grow, their wings will glide
in great arches, like the naves of cathedrals.
I don't understand their sharp squawks.
I only know that a reckoning is coming
and that I, too, will be required to confess.

PANIC ATTACK

My mind begins to rhyme.
Gift remiss thrift bliss—
I can't stop the words
from stuttering themselves.
Tunnel, kennel, funnel, runnel.
My mind's unpinned.
There's a spinning in my brain.
A whirl in my sight.
I hear my voice a moment
after I've spoken—my memory's
broken. Repeating myself,
my voice and feet stumble.
What I say gets lost in a mire.
Dear God, this tongue,
this mumble, this not-me,
this getting up and sitting down,
getting up and sitting down.
There's no end to it.
I pack a bag for the hospital.
Arrange carefully:
my shoes, tooth brush,
pajamas. I await the moment
when my heart will overheat,
when my lungs will erupt
with blood and lack of breath.
I'm patient. I wait.
There's a sack of grain on my chest.
There's a clot in my veins.
There's a lack of sense
in my brain. *Shoes, blue, you.*
I'm a stream, a dam, I'm damned.
My dead father walks into the room.

Free of time from time free.
Heard knells from the hills.
Give me a pill to stop who I am.

KLONOPINE

> To die will be an awfully big adventure!
> —JAMES BARRIE, *PETER PAN*

One pill and a half each night. I bite
a scored mint-green tablet and tilt
my head beneath the faucet to wash
down smoothly the chalky bitten edge.
How gradually it brings me calm,
like the mother who straightens
her children's littered minds at night,
neatly folding memories, sorting
them into piles, crumpling as trash
whatever might sharpen the corners
of sleep and wake a child in worry.

Oh, I'm not sorry to lose my shadow,
Peter Pan. I've swallowed
the ticking clock myself, I hear it
all day long, its muffled minute hand
beating inside me like a second heart.
But now, as I lie down, windows open,
I fear nothing, hear nothing, pillow
my head in a haze of lovely ease.
All the papers in my brain unmoor,
and whatever shore to which I fly
tonight will be empty, silent as thread,
and no alarm, until I wake, will harm me.

UNFINISHED

for Kiwana Thomas Gayden (1975–2018)

Friday night, you checked into the hospital.
The next Thursday you died: I'll never know
exactly why, and there's no one to ask.
Your grieving husband, your mother?
Cancer threw you down gasping and clammy.
I heave at the news that you're gone.
A friend tells me your work on earth
was finished, God took you home to be whole.
Be at peace, she tells me. *Seek.*
But you were not finished—
you still had books you meant to read,
and shows to watch, beads to string
with your chemo-numbed fingers.

Not knowing you, my mother bought me a painting
of a Gullah woman named Emma, turbaned,
the background hue mustard yellow, your favorite.
You were determined to go to South Carolina,
you told me, for a Gullah festival.
That, too, never happened.
The painting, my mother pointed out, is unfinished—
the woman's body reduced, in the bottom right corner,
to mere stripes of paint and penciled outline.
I'm glad it's incomplete.

In your last message to me,
you said you were going to nap
and I wrote, *OK, sleep well,*
I love you, and you wrote,
I'll talk to you tomorrow, love you too.
And then everything, always, unfinished.

METASTATIC

I'd like a long braid to lasso my rage away,
to stand on a stage in a garter belt
and thigh-high boots and stamp my feet
through the floor, like to put my face
right up against someone else's face and scream
until the scream knocks me to my knees, coughing.
I could become an arsonist, delicious click of the lighter.
Every time someone I love dies, I'd like a diamond
to line the hilt of a dagger, or tip an arrow.
I'd like to shoot the whole God-damned universe
through its infinite starry center, and watch it suck
into itself, scattering the suns and galaxies
over each other like a jar of tipped glitter.
Don't tell me not to be angry. Do you know
how close I am to flinging my whole body
at you, how little I care about being hit
back or spat on, or bruised? Humiliation
means nothing to me. I have nothing to lose.
If you push me off a building, I'll sing.
I'd jump in front of a bullet if I could.
I'd let someone wring my neck if only
I knew it would hurt God just one bit to watch me die.

CROW'S FUNERAL

> Crows have been observed gathering around the bodies
> of dead crows, sounding calls of panic.

When I die, throw me a crow's funeral.
No eulogy, no poems or psalms.
Leave behind the candles and hymns,
the hypnotic chants at vespers,
the bound and hammered hands of Christ.
Let the company assemble outside,
bare-headed beneath the sky,
weeds and dirt the only altar cloths,
the dying oak, still rooted in the soil,
casting a chuppah for the Shekinah.
Cluster, beloveds, around my urn.
Then, in turn, mimic the outraged
cries of crows, their shrieks for the dead.
Scream until alarmed birds rise,
bowing a black shroud, a rent,
a tent to accept my soul.

ACKNOWLEDGMENTS

THE WEEK ANYA DIED, she had planned to send out her newly finished manuscript to me and her friends in the poetry community. Her manuscript was still open on her computer when I returned home from the hospital. I read many of these poems for the first time on that day.

I edited the final version of the manuscript with the generous and wise counsel of my coeditor, Laurie Watel, who was instrumental in the shaping of this book, and whose love of Anya and her poetry helped sustain me in the months after Anya's death. I cannot put into words how thankful I am for her friendship and how thankful I am for her guidance, judgment, and devotion to Anya's work. This manuscript owes so much to Laurie Watel's care and wisdom.

I'm indebted too to a team of poets who lent their feedback to the project, including Stephen Bluestone, who painstakingly and adoringly reviewed every poem of Anya's that I assembled for him in the weeks after her death, along with Nicole Cooley, who offered guidance every step of the way. Sara Pirkle, Kevin Cantwell, Barbara Crooker, and Julie Moore also gave crucial feedback and insights about the manuscript.

Anya would have also warmly thanked the Guggenheim committee for selecting her for a fellowship the year that she died. It was the honor of her life to receive the award. "Beyond my wildest dreams," she wrote.

Much thanks too for the patience and encouragement of LSU Press, as Anya has put it before, "for trusting my work and for bringing it to an audience." As I've grieved these past years, LSU has been a steadfast champion of Anya's work. Thanks especially to Neal Novak for his patience and eagle eye in the editing process.

Thanks to Mercer University for supporting Anya's work through her years of teaching and writing, and thanks to President Bill Underwood for generously supporting the development of this manuscript.

Anya would have thanked her closest friends, Ellen Byron, Sarah Gerwig, and Oonie Lynch—she'd have called them "guardian angels"—for their love and support while writing these poems. She would also have sent her love to Ellen's two young daughters, Grace and Julia, both of whom adored Anya and began forays into poetry themselves.

Though her friends gave her much-needed love, her sisters in the metastatic community gave her love alongside the complete understanding of an illness they themselves experience daily. I cannot overstate the importance of the metastatic breast cancer community in Anya's life, but they were her lifeline, her ministers, her congregation, and, more often than not, her nurses, her physician's assistants, and her doctors. I knew how much the community meant to her while she lived, but I realized only after she died how much her voice meant to this community. In particular, her friendship with Kiwana Gayden sustained her in her last year, and Kiwana's death left her inconsolable just a month before she died. Others in the metastatic community have helped both Anya and me these past years include Ginny Mason, Abigail Johnston, Emily Garnett, Julia Maues, Christine Hodgdon, Terlisa Sheppard, Kelly Shanahan, Janice Cowden, Natalia Padron, Susan Rahn, Jersi Baker, Marina Pomare Kaplan, and too many others to name.

ANYA ALWAYS CLOSED HER acknowledgements with notes to her family. She would have thanked her mother, Christel, whom she adored and who brought her love, relaxation, and comfort—a kind of space apart from illness—every time she visited. And she would have thanked her father for encouraging her poetry and for cultivating her desire for the beautiful, the good, and the true. And she would have thanked her beloved sister, Claudia Krugovoy, her lifelong best friend, who has lived through the loss of her husband this last year without her sister's love and support. I hope, dear Claudia, that you can feel Anya with you in these poems.

Anya would have thanked last, because his life was her fondest wish, our son Noah. She told him that nothing she accomplished in life "is equal to your birth." In the posthumous letter she left Noah, she wrote: "What I want you to know the most is how very much I love you, that being your mom is the most important thing I've ever done, and that I will love you forever and always be your mom." She ended the letter: "I still exist. Energy doesn't die. Think of the soul as energy."

I'm grateful for the twenty-three years that Anya and I walked through this life in love as soulmates together, and I'm grateful for all of the readers who love Anya's poetry as much as I do. Anya did not get to hold this book in her hands, but every word in this book is a witness, music before the silence coming.

—ANDREW SILVER

www.ingramcontent.com/pod-product-compliance
Lightning Source LLC
Chambersburg PA
CBHW030123170426
43198CB00009B/715